T0380959

Stations

JOHN F. KUMMER

To order additional copies of this book, contact:
Xlibris
1-888-795-4274
www.Xlibris.com
Orders@Xlibris.com

ISBN: Softcover   978-1-7960-8118-3
        Hardcover   978-1-7960-8119-0
        EBook   978-1-7960-8117-6

Print information available on the last page

Rev. date: 01/23/2020

PREFIX

"Resurrection"

Oh the joy of resurrection!
      The moment of life anew;
            the end of this world
                  the beginning of the next.
      The Beatific Vision;
         God and us together complete.

Resurrection
      to rise from "death";
            life with new "breath"
              From utter demise
               to once again new life.
What was lifeless now has being.
         What was without being now has existence.
But not a Frankenstein,
      from the dead revived;
          not some body contrived.
              Not some creature ghoulish;
                nothing so foolish.

But to have life to its fullness.
        Have being to its completeness.
"Resuscitation" but more.
        To the next "world" life restore.
           From temporary life here
                to life permanent there.

Yet, does one have to wait
        this world end,
          the flavor of resurrection to taste;
        this life to close
          another life to experience?
Lazarus from the dead raised,
        not to the next world come,
          but to this world once more.
The widow's son deceased;
        once more to his mother returned.
          The little girl "sleeping"
            to her parents awakened.
All revived from death,
        only again later to die.
          Resurrected for now
           only later to "sleep" fully.
Is this not also resurrection?
        Is this not also rebirth and new life?

For one does not need wait
                until life over
                            to savor resurrection.
        one does not need die physically
                            resurrection to have affect.
In this life also
        resurrection takes place;
                    New birth can occur.
                            Renewed life happens.
How could any one
            from death
            to this world returned
                        not feel a wonder;
                            not undergo awe?
        For not just in the eternal
                but also in the finite.
But, resurrecting
        not necessarily
            a pretty word
                or romantic thought.
Resurrecting
    not instantaneous
            or spontaneous.
It is not inevitable,
        sudden glorification
                or instant purification.
Resurrecting in this life
            can be slow and often tedious;
                    painful and even imperceptible.

It often happens gradually,
                inconsistently,
                        "un-surely",
                                hesitantly.
The wandering son to his father returns
                and is "raised up" and restored.
                                        Not easily.
                                Not comfortably.
                                But restored.

From despair once more hope.
                From grief and doubt once more life.
                        From addiction and fears, courage to face.
These, too, are a form of resurrection;
                                life renewed.

For Jesus, the man,
                resurrecting began
                        long before His crucifixion;
                                long before He
                                        on the cross died.
It began
    in a manger;
                in a stable;
                        under a star.
                                with Mary,
                                        with Joseph.
It began with angels and song.
                With shepherds and sheep.
                        With Magi and gifts.

With us, too,
        upon our birth,
                we begin to find our way.
With our first breath
        God's will to fulfill.
                Ourselves fully become.
For resurrecting
        not just physical;
                it is also spiritual.
                        Not just "bodily"
                                but also "mystically".
It is our soul
        being called into relationship;
                our heart being summoned into love.
It is a process
        of self awareness;
                a progression
                        of self discovery.
Jesus spent His life
        answering His Father's call.

                He gave His life
                        fulfilling God's summon.
And we too are commanded;
                to do the same;
                to unveil who God
                        would like us to be.
                To discover that person
                        God created us to be.

However, as Lazarus,
    from the tomb came out,
        when summoned,
            so too, we on our own
                from ourselves, forth must come.
As the young man and girl
    answered Jesus' call,
        so to must we respond.
           Repeated conversion
        to Jesus' voice repeated. And
here the challenge;
    here the heavy stone.
        For within us the tomb.
           Within us the grave.
And a far darker tomb
    than the earth;
      a deeper grave
        than any hole dug.
It is from here
  that the way of the cross begins.
             It is from here
        the path to resurrection starts.
From this spot
  the via dolorous begins.
        No shortcuts.
         No free rides.

It can be scary.
        It can be fretful.
                It can be daunting.
                        But the freedom to be found
                                when our true selves
                                        forth come as God intended.
                                when God's true creations
                                        can be seen and appreciated.
Repeated resurrection this world
        until the final resurrection in the next.

But, do I
        the courage have
                        to let God lead?
                                Do I the faith
                                        His steps to follow?
At station one,
                step one;
                        at station fifteen
                                        the rest
                                                of the journey.
Jesus the path has shown.
                Christ the-way has gone.
My resurrections await
                my awakenings loom.
                                Can I answer
                                        God's call for me?
                                                Can I from my "grave" step?
                                                        In renewed life breath?

PROLOGUE

"Bottom Line"

There is
   a bottom line
      to life;
        a bottom line
          to living.
It's that fine print
   that defines who I am.
      That point of focus
        that states my being.
It is that key
   that unlocks my desires
      and incites my actions.
        It is that catalyst
          that stirs my interests
            and excites my reactions.
It is what
   after all done
      and said
        is the candor
          of my soul.

after all
    stripped
        and bared
            is the marrow
                of my ego.
It is the reason
    for my moods.
        The why
            for my attitudes.

And never may
    I know what is that true line;
        where lies that center spine.
            But exist it does
                It is my because.
It may be hidden
    in various disguises;
        dead ends and false surmises,
            There will be changing mazes
                and thinking hazes.
What you think
    the bottom line is factually
        may not be actually.
        For it can fluctuate and mutate.
            It can modulate and vacillate.
        Like a virus our health infects,
            so too this bottom line
                your thinking affects.

Yet, it is what influences
        my perception of God.
                What colors my understanding
                        of self.
It is what guides me
        in my relationships
                and impacts my fellowships.
It is the slab
      of cement
          in which all else
               is set firm.
               In which all else
                   has little squirm.

Find that bottom line
        and find your core.
             Find that bottom line
                and find your soul's mentor.
Be it fear.
    Be it hurt.
      Be it joy.
        Be it grief
         Be it love.
          Be it hate.
          Be it what-ever.

It can be a "thief".
  For it filters
   all we do.
    It tints
    all we are.
     Even our faith
      it can alter.
       Our feelings halter.
Without our knowing;
  without our awareness;
   our lives it can control.
    Our living, it can ensnare us.
And like a statue
  in a stone,
   longs to be found;
    so our true selves
     long to be unbound.
      Ever so gradually;
       ever so crudely.
Each of us struggling
  to be clear of our confinement.

   Each of us reaching out
     to be loose of our "define-ment".
During life, bit by bit
  we learn our wills to adjust.
   Little by little, we learn
    who or what to trust.
We self analyze and philosophize.
  We religious-size and vocalize.

We pray as Paul,
        that the "thorn from my side"
                be deleted.
                    That one day,
                        that ache inside,
                            be depleted.

Our faults we confess
        with no permanent success.
                We say, 'that is me and who I be.
                        Never perfect me'.
        So, with that "separation" still dealt.
                        Within us that welt;
                            that kernel still felt.

So we live as imperfect creatures
        with our imperfect features.
                Trying to love ourselves
                    so we can love our neighbors.

Never quite understanding,
        who we fully are.
                Never feeling completely at home
                    with where we are.

There is
    a bottom line
        to life;

            a bottom line
                to living.
It's that fine print
        that defines who I am.
                That point of focus
                that states my being.

With that we have
        to learn to live with.
                With that we have
                        to come to terms with.

Even though God sees
        the finished stone;
                we only the scratches
                        and roughness prone.
                                But unfinished statues
                                        a deep beauty
                                                of their own.
                                Their own persona;
                                        statues rough hon.

Jesus, His bottom line clear;
        faith for His Father not veer.

Station I
Jesus is Condemned

"Judgment"

Before my mother I stand
      with sweating hand;
            Before my dad I wait
                wondering of my fate.
Before my teacher I sweat,
      dreading the grade I get.
             Before the interviewer I sit,
                hoping this job I fit.
So through the days
      my life decided many ways.
             Judged in some form
                by some decided norm.
Sometimes the outcome already known;
      hopes and results already blown.
             A shot in blindness;
                praying for kindness. Dd
Other times, perhaps, better connected;
      chance I have to be accepted.
             There are times, when even favored
                and being chosen savored.

Judgment a part of living.
    Judgment a natural giving.
        With every choice we make
            a judgment it does take.
If one chosen another rejected;
    If one rejected another chosen.
        A constant process of weighing;
            An ongoing stream of assaying.
Sometimes with objectivity.
    Other time pure subjectivity.
        Sometimes thought well out.
            Other times not thought about.
Preconceived, my decisions set.
    Maybe a sense of threat.
        Perhaps clear cut my view;
            perhaps at times, eschew.
Hopefully, balanced my thinking;
    with little shrinking.
        Biases kept from conveying;
            Prejudices kept from swaying.
Of course hard that path to stay;
    always a little convey and sway.
        Still I try when deciding;

        and the "fence" I am riding
            to keep from distortion sliding.
And in everything we judge:
    From the everyday to the mainstay.
    From the "simplex" to the complex.
        From playing to praying
            From retreating to proceeding.

But with people a different story;
much more hoary.
A different perspective.
A greater reflective.
More care to be taken.
More concern to be awaken.

Yet often, others I have judged
with little regard to fact;
condemned with careless tact.
I have incriminated
with "un-right" sight;
have discriminated with blind mind.

More time have I spent
on a shirt selecting
than on a person's life reflecting.
More time a menu wondering
than someone's life pondering.

And not only on others
my hasty declaration;
but upon myself also
a swift citation.
For many scars have I from self accusation.
Many wounds have I from self denunciation.

The voice within my head
a yelling thong.
Within my soul, Pilate's voice
saying get along.
Its mind set;
Its verdict passed.

No compassion due;
No mercy accrued.
And for my crown of thorns:
shame and scorn.

For as in the skin
      stings the nettle
          so to in our soul guilt can settle.
              An irritation beneath the seeing;
                  a self reproach within our being.
And not easy the soothing;

      not quickly the smoothing.
          For some, even harder the healing;
              for some, even harder the feeling.
Yet, unlike the Passion,
      Jesus on the bench resides.
          Unlike Pilate,
              Christ the "judge" presides.
And He, my voice defies;
      He, the throng's wishes denies.
          And even though I object
              my words He does reject.
                  With stern reprimand,
                    He leaves the stand.
"Go and do as I have done to you.
      Where forgiveness needed; forgive.
      Where exoneration due; exonerate.
          And not just on others
              but yourself too;
                For to love another
                  first love you.

For every judgment given
        a judgment on two.
           a judgment on the other
              a judgment on you."
Easier to expound than to enact.
        Easier to just react.
         For first remove the nettle.
           This alone can test your mettle.
      Only then can the stinging subside.
          Only then can the healing in inside.

Though no facts incriminating;
      Jesus' guilt still insinuating.
        His blamelessness discarded.
         His innocence disregarded.
           His cross His sentence.
             His death our penitence.

Station II
Jesus Picks Up Cross

"Procrastination"

Procrastination a long word;
  a fancy sounding word.
   A word harder to say than to do
     since you "never" have to do.
A favorite word for many students;
  a well practiced word by others.
    Useful in any pinch to buy time;
     a means to tweak time.
For procrastination is
  the art of putting off;
   doing "later" what could be done "now".
    The science of doing "tomorrow"
     what should be done "today".
You take "now" and move to "later";
  You take "today" and make it "tomorrow".
   A form of time travel in ones mind.
    "Now" is rescheduled for "later";
     And "today" becomes "tomorrow".

A simple time switch;
      an "inter-time" change,
            that can amazingly be
                  repeated numerous times.
                        Until "today" can become a vague "future".
                                And "now" turns into "whenever".
                                        A trick of the mind.
                                          A slight of clock.

But the cool thing
      is that whenever done
            it will still be "today"
                and will still be "now".
Perhaps a little confusing
        when being explained.
            Hard to put into words the finesse
                of the manipulation of time.

To the outsider
      it looks like foolishness.
            But if properly done,
              what needed doing,
                may no longer need to be done.
                    Or already done by another.

No, procrastination
      not an easy word to say

            or even to spell,
                but it is a natural talent
                    that the young pick up early.
                        and with age it is fine honed.

And having been a student
    of procrastination for some time;
        and having some experience in it;
            I can do it casually without thought;
                I can be formal in planning;
                    I can be theatrical.
                        I can be mercy pleading.

It can become second nature;
    a part of my daily being.
        For procrastination addictive;
            quite habit forming.
                Once tried and succeeded,
                    hard to resist doing again.
And it is astounding what can be put off
    to "manana", "tomorrow", "later".
        What can be pushed to the edge;
            at the last second done.
  Many a homework assignment
    last moment finished.
        Many a chore
          last second completed.
            Many a tax return
              final moment filed.

And the more time to do
    the longer put off;
        the more time given
        the greater the time waited.

This is especially true
        of those things long avoided;
                no desire to do;
              of those things dreaded,
                  long circumvented;
                     of those things feared,
                       at all costs long evaded.
          Those things the heart
              does not want to handle.
For there are very few of us,
      who do not put off something
          regardless the reason.
         Be it medical appointments.

              Be it personal problems.
                Be it financial concerns.
All of us, in our own way,
      procrastinate.
        We all have that "item"
          not yet ready to face
That "cross" not, yet,
      ready to accept.
        That part of us not ready
          to be dealt with.
        That part hidden;
         tucked away from even our own thought.

There are, however, some things
        that cannot be avoided.
            That must be faced and taken care of.
              That sooner or later demand attention.
If it be ones own death,
        no way to get around it,
            If it be facing a fear,
              no longer put off.
                If it be family feud long lasting,
                    now needed to address.

For a "cross" long carried,
        heavier the weight.
            The longer ignored,
              the more it festers and pains.
                Until finally, it cannot be any further bared.
                    It cannot any longer be put off.

But for now, whatever it be
        manana, manana, manana!
            Tomorrow, tomorrow, tomorrow!

Jesus, to Jerusalem went,
        there a cross to receive.
            No procrastination.
              No putting off what needed to be done.
                He put His shoulder to it
                  and "carried" it.
What love can do.
        What love can endure.

Station III
Jesus First Fall

"Falling"

A good deal
        of my childhood
                falling was spent.
                        A goodly amount of time
                                to the ground I went.
With scraped skin
        and banged chin;
                with bruises redundant
                        and cuts abundant;
                                with knees red
                                        elbows bled.
All the toll of a child
        running about.
                All the cost of gravity
                        experimenting.
And though
        not always vigilant,
                nor always prudent;
                        Not always forethought
                                nor even afterthought.

Still in between the scrapes,
a feeling of accomplishment.
In spite of the bruises,
a sense of achievement.

For the fun
was worth the hurt.
The adventures
worth the discomfort.
Maybe not right then,
but always soon
something else again.

The pain was typical.
The cuts and gashes habitual.
A part of daily play.
A part of the childhood melee.

And if in action,
a spill extraordinaire,
once mended,
physics again would dare.
For a setback never a stay back.
A fall taken never the spirit shaken.

And into the imagination wild
runs once more the child.
A world of fantasy
and make believe;
a world where
anything can be conceived.

A world that slowly fades
and eventually "reality" invades.
But for a time enchanted,
a youngster's heart granted.

With age, however,
      more cautious am I.
         With the years,
           more considerate
              of limb and eye.
Still now and then,
      a tumble I take.
         Once in awhile
           still a stumble I make.
              But fewer they are
                and in between far.
Yet, with every "knee" scraped
      the slower I heal.
         With every "elbow" taped
           the more pain I feel.
And as with my body,
      so too, my heart and soul.
         For they, too,
           their trips have had.
              For many a tender sore;
                many a lesion not wished for.
With each wound
      a lesson learned.
         With each abrasion
         a memory burned.
            Not always kind.
            Not always benign.
Therefore, a more protective heart
      inside deep.
         A more guarded spirit within
           I now keep.

For once love put into gear
       the outcome not always clear.
            Once, love begun
               hard to be undone.
Yet, too, only by doing
       will I ever acquire

           that which we all desire.
             That which we require,
               love to aspire.
But in the process
       a daring heart must I possess.
          And when on the ground I land
            and I don't think I can "re-stand",
Once more the child's soul
       I need to show.
         That youngster's spunk
           needs to be "thunk".
            Once more, that God given spirit
               I need to "re-stir".

Jesus on His Father's Spirit relied.
       Again His Father did He confide
          Once more another stride.

STATION IV
JESUS MEETS HIS MOTHER

How Long?

How long
    must one hold
        a dying friend's hand,
            a lifetime to last?
How long
    must one kiss
        a dying loved one' face
            to keep that kiss alive
                for the days ahead?

How long
    must one study
        a loved one's face
            to keep in your mind
                forever encased?
How do you let go
        of a dying person
            and yet recall
                his or her feel;
                  his or her smell?

How do you preserve
         a loved one's touch,
                  a loved one's closeness,
                           a loved one's spirit?
         So always there
                  with you
                           when he or she
                                    no longer is?
Will photographs
         and portraits

                  on tables and walls
                           the memory keep in tact?
Or will items,
         once by them touched,
                  remind us when
                           we in turn touch them
                                    and hold them close?
 Or can we the nearness save
                  with letters or notes
                           written and signed;
                                    the person's name bearing?
Perhaps, if all else fails,
         a voice recording
                  the feelings will renew?
                           The sound of their talk
                                    and inflections
                                             will again remind?
         Or a video,
                  action and movement,
                           sight and sound
                                    will once more
                                             new life give to them?

Still these are
          but "relics",
                    bits and pieces
                              of a life now changed;
                                        a person now moved on.
Even, if a room preserved,
                    as was when last
                              the person lived,
                                        all you have is
                                                  a mausoleum
                                                            and nothing more.

For it is a vain attempt
                    to hold tightly
                              to what cannot be held.
                                        To try to save
                                                  what cannot be saved.
Yet, still the effort given
                    for one's heart
                              to not lose completely
                                        what is already fading.
               A deep felt desire
                    to not discard fully
                              what is so quickly receding.
But memory is not the present,
                    but a shadow,
                              lacking any breath of life;
                    a faint image,
                              devoid of any sign of being.

Perhaps then
    we are not meant
        to keep someone "alive"
            in this world
                when he or she is
                    now in the next.
Perhaps, we
    are now asked
        not to cling,
          but to let
            be free
              in order
                for us to be free.
And then the memory
    can be a gentle current

        in our hearts
           that reminds us of our love;
       a sweet sad undertow of recall
           at those times of deja vu.
       of unexpected recollection.
Yes, all attempts to keep alive
      the touch and feel
        of a cherished soul
          is but a poor hope;
            a weak endeavor.
For photos and such,
    theft and fire;
      lost and destruction
        can claim.

Same too recordings and videos,
　　　　letters and "relics"
　　　　　　so easily vanished;
　　　　　　　　so easily
　　　　　　　　　　from us taken.

 Even our own mind
　　　　through time
　　　　　　can fail us.
　　　　　　　Even our brain
　　　　　　　　through time
　　　　　　　　　can forget.

So once more I ask;
　　　　once more I wonder.
How long
　　must one hold
　　　　a dying friend's hand
　　　　　　a lifetime to last?
How long
　　must one kiss

　　　　a dying loved one' face
　　　　　　to keep that kiss alive
　　　　　　　for the days ahead?

How long
　　must one study
　　　　a loved one's face
　　　　　　to keep in your mind
　　　　　　　forever encased?
There is no answer;
　　　only a wish
　　　　to never let go;
　　　　　only a need
　　　　　　to never stop;

But, we have to do both
                in order to go on;
                        and so we do;
                                for there is
                                        never enough time,
                                                never enough life,
                                                        never enough love.

Only in the heart
        can a loved one
                be kept safe;
                        imperfectly but kept.
Only in the heart stored;
        incompletely, but stored;
                with that hope one day restored.
                                One day together again.

Mary had to let Jesus pass;
        with her grief to contend.
                Jesus, His mother, had to leave;

                                With His sorrow,
                                        cross to still carry.

STATION V
JESUS CARRIES HIS CROSS

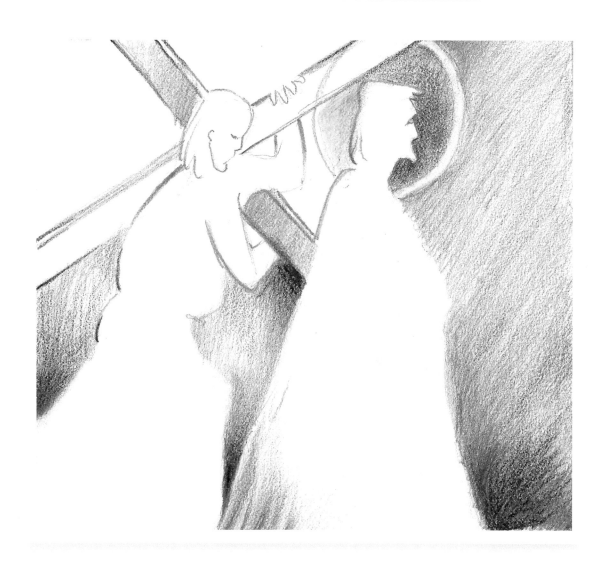

"Simon"

When I, a youngster was,
> for many a thing blamed was I.
>> Most times correctly so.
>>> Other times the verdict awry.

For sometimes for another
> on me the fault laid.
>> Innocent though I was,
>>> still the penalty paid.
>>>> I, a lad so sweet,
>>>>> this way the world to treat.

And no matter the tearful pleading,
> my innocence not heeding.
>> So I, the punishment took,
>>> while another escaped the hook.

And I will admit that I too
> at times set free,
>> while another the blame
>>> suffered for me.

And bravely forward I did not not leap;
   myself I did not offer in a sorrowful heap,
      but mum I remained;
        my innocence feigned.

So even now goes it on.
   Sometimes the innocent
     the burden take;
      while the guilty the burden shake.
And we in turn our burdens
   onto another back
    we try to place.
     Hoping they, for us,
      the load will embrace.
But we hope not only the task will they take,
   but also the pain and the ache.
So ask I now whose burden do I carry?

Whose cross on my shoulders do I ferry?
   No name on it anywhere around.
     No identification to be found.
Could I the wrong cross be claiming?
   The wrong burden misnaming?
     For so many burdens existing,
      hard the ownership to tell.
       Difficult to separate them well.
What if this another person's cross
   that I juggle;
    what a waste of time and struggle.
     All these blisters for naught
      All these calluses for no fault.

Do I carry it out of "guilt"
        from my emotional quilt?
           Or do I out of duty with it trudge
               to please an inner judge?
                  Or do I out of love this cross lift
                     as if a precious gift

Why even with this cross do I toil?
        Am I to a code being loyal?
        Trying not an image to spoil?
          To me this burden entrusted
             or on me was it "thrust-ed"?
So again the question is inquired,
        whose cross is this that I acquired?
          Is it of my own doing
            or have others helped in its gluing?

Is it for me alone to bear
        or do others in it share?
          A community care
           or an individual affair?
Jesus' cross Simon helped carry,
        but it was not voluntary.
          No help did he offer.
           No aid did he proffer;
             but by force demanded;
               by the Romans commanded.
With a cross not his own,
        Simon to Golgotha went;
          under the beam weight bent.
            To Calvary the cross with Jesus "brung",
              but on it who would be hung?

On Golgotha two strangers stood?
　　　　　Two men and a cross of wood

　　　　　　　For whom was it intended?
　　　　　　　　　Who upon it would be appended?

Two men Golgotha ascended.
　　　Only one man Golgotha descended.
　　　　Two men with a cross of wood travailed,
　　　　　　but only one man on the cross nailed.
　　　　　　　　One man on Golgotha remained
　　　　　　　　　The other no longer restrained
At day's end
　　with his life to contend
　　　　what did Simon feel
　　　　　about the whole ordeal?
Relieved was he now from the scene away
　　　　or did he in his mind the moment replay;
　　　　　　wondering why that way home he came.
　　　　　　　Wondering if he would ever be the same.
Always on Golgotha two people stood
　　　　between them a cross of wood..
　　　　　　Was it Jesus' cross to claim?
　　　　　Or was it to his own cross Simon came?
　　　　　　　Or on it, is each our own name?

STATION VI
VERONICA WIPES JESUS FACE

"Can Still Be Seen"

As light from a distant star,
        long time ago given off, can still be seen;
Even though that particular sun
          might now be dead and dark;
Just as true,
   a deed of charity,
       no matter when done,
        its own light can still be observed.
A word of kindness,
      even though forgotten,
        its effects can still be felt.
Sometimes even unknown
     the moment when the deed done.
        Sometimes no longer even recalled
         who the kindness expressed.
Yet, that deed a life of its own;
     that kindness it retains.
      For no love squandered,
        no caring wasted.

As that dead star's radiance
        still travels forth;
            So the work of the breathing Spirit
                does not cease, but continues outward.
As that dormant sun's
        once brightness yet shines;
            So God's living Word radiates out
                and cannot be stopped,
Either by time
    or distance;
        by fear or by "blindness".
            For God's love knows no boundaries;
                the Spirit's grace
                    has no limitations.

The deeds that we do
      in God's name,
          after us
            can still animate;
              can still vitalize our spirits.
The kindness that we show in faith,
        after we, too, in this, world dead

                can still produce light
                  and hope.

Veronica, Jesus' face does wipe
      and on her cloth, His image remains.
           So too, of those we help,
              on us their images remain.

"Thumbprints"

Upon my soul
        many a thumbprint lays;
             many a finger has touched.
                  Many a hand has felt.
For no one comes or goes,
        who touches me in some way so.
               For I am all I have met;
                  I am all I have known.
In me, each a mark has left.
       In me, each own way lives.
          I am a living painting
             of voices and faces.
                A breathing portrait
                  of people and places.
And in them too,
       my own marks have I left.
          In them too, my own thumbprints lay.
             In creation have we
               a hand shared.
                Each others' lives
                  have we help fashion.

So be aware of those

        whom you touch;

                of what you say and do.

                        Remember we all leave prints.

                                Our own marks, we all produce.

Will it be for the better

            or for the worse?

                  Will it be positive

                        or negative?

Christ's Gospel will we share

            or will, we, His Word forbear?

                  With each meeting

                      one of the two.

                        With each greeting

                            one or the other.

Station VII
Jesus Falls Again

"Regrets"

Many a thing
    I've done
      regret has resulted
        Many a thing
          I've not done
            regret has resulted
    And now
      as my life
        I survey
          The stories
            and events
              I purvey

      many an interruption
        many a disruption
          many a disconnection
            many a dissection
And as potholes
    a road disrepair
      so do these "regrets"
        my life impair
Some my own initiating
      Others
        another's instigating

Still all

in my heart abiding

All within me hiding

And many a form

does regret masquerade

Various disguises

does it parade

Sometime as guilt

comes it concealed

with wagging finger

blaming eyes

revealed

At times different

shame the hidden face

with nagging voice

ongoing disgrace

But regret

even a more subtle abode

A more persistent mode

Disappointment endless

Sadness ceasless

Source not

always evident

Origin not

always definite

An unsure depression

An unknown repression

So regrets
        beneath the spirit pester
                As chiggers
                        in the flesh fester
And though some regrets
            their resolving provide
                    Most regrets
                            leave one stupefied
                                    and hogtied
                No seeming way
                            to rectify
                            No seeming way
                                        to nullify
                    Any chance blown
                            Any opportune flown
                As a well said word
                            never said
                As a well done deed
                            never done
                For time now
                        out of synch
                Circumstances
                    no longer in link
And even if
        correct I could
            I doubt if I would
                For too long ago
                        the happening
                    Too long ago
                            the occurring
                                No longer
                                    the connection
                                Now a different
                                        direction

So remorse

an emptiness

sustains

An uncertainty

a numbness

engrains

Like Novocain

pain dulls

so misgivings

self trust nulls

For what

once seemed right

now erroneous appears

what

once seemed best

now the opposite veers

Yet, a decision

I did decide

An action

I justified

And now

with it

I must reside

For second guessing

is an abyss

without light

or sight

A chasm

without sound

or ground

For doubt a dim lamp

with little shine

Regret a poor trail

with no dotted line

So accept regrets
              I must
                   Within my soul
                           they rust
                                a part of
                                     my permanent profile
                                              a part of
                                                   my concluding file
And though
        I patch
            and repatch
                   where I am able
                           Most of these flaws
                                       and holes
                                           remain unstable
And though
        I repair
              and pave
                   Mend
                      and slave
                          I realize
                              the road
                                  never again
                                       level will be
                                           Never again
                                               from debris free
But that shows
            it is a road
                well trekked
                    if not well laid
                       A byway
                            well traversed

                                    if not well paved

Station VIII
Jesus Meets the Women

"Interaction"

Sometimes a great incident occurs
                our world to agitate.
                  Other times, but a tiny event;
                      an awareness to generate.
It can be global,
    our lives to perturb.
        It can be personal,
            our beings disturb.
If impact slight,
    we pay but little heeding.
           Our daily lives
               on own proceeding.
If effect severe,
    our focus interrupted.
        Our daily lives,
           a sudden disrupted.
The same when a person stumbles.
        The selfsame effect.
          When someone tumbles,
             another person the outcome affect.

For when someone falters;
        another life it somehow alters.
                When one life does change,
                      another life it can rearrange.
It may be physical or emotional.
        It can be psychological
                or "commotional".
              It may be obvious
                      or almost oblivious.
                            It may be grieved
                              or barely perceived.
The impact may reverberate
            or barley vibrate.
                An earthquake rumbling
                    or just a tremor grumbling.
But in some way or fashion
            to another comes the reaction;
                  in some way an interaction;
                        no matter the brevity
                            or the longevity.

For no one so isolated
      that, from others, completely insulated.
                No one into a void born.
                  No one, from others, totally "shorn".
From conception, each of us
            of others composed.
                From moment of birth,
                  our lives interposed.
And our lives throughout,
      with others interaction and reaction.
                With those people about,
                  satisfaction or friction.

We are individuals in "community" dwelling;
in population swelling.
Longing a place for our self.
Yearning a space for myself.
We may try to be aloof.
Indifference be our roof.
From others stay apart..
from others keep out heart.
But, we all have a need to communicate;
a need to collaborate.
And even at times
a need to celebrate.
For we too, with other souls a connection;
someone else for affection.
For we are in varied ways entwined.
An unseen twine our lives bind.
For a distinct few direct;
For the rest a general connect.
And for the most part, a breath taken,
the world never shaken.
Still, a bit of air now changed;
for carbon dioxide exchanged.
But, if within a small space confined,
each breath can be defined.
And if air "limitive"
each breath more definitive.
And if others the air to share,
less air soon aware.

Breathing now a chore;
air getting poor.
A change of circumstance
a different stance.
What was once presumed;
now no longer assumed.
Thus the world

all of us pulls in;
to some degree therein.
Even if unaware,
the effect there.
The more direct the impact
the more the dealing.
The farther from us
less the feeling.

Jesus to the women speaks,
but not their comfort does He seek.
Instead, a warning does He give
of the future they will live.
How their lives too will be touched
by the world surrounding.
How suffering they too will feel;
by the world rebounding.

Station IX
Jesus Falls the Third Time

"Decisions"

I have left many a decision dangling.
Varied choices wrangling.
A mobile tangling.
I have left decisions pending.
Plans left suspending.
No sure choice.
No clear voice.
And more the thought;
more the distraught.
The more indecisive,
more divisive.
Never ending debate;
procrastinate.
Thick smoke,
myself to cloak.

Fear of a mistake,
no risk I take.
Fear position wrong,
I do not stay strong.
Fear of consequences resulting.
Fear later doubting.

Most decisions though
        no thought given;
                of their own absently driven.
                        But, other decisions greater pondering;
                                more conscientious wandering.
And even with prayer.
        still sense of despair.
                God's voice not clear.
                        His answer, I not hear.
For some decisions deciding,
        tough the abiding.
                Others once beget,
                        hard to reset.
For some no turning back.
        For some no backtrack.
                Too late the rehearsing.
                    To far come for reversing.
For once in action,

        hard retraction.
            Once in motion,
                hard to stop locomotion.
Once from tree house jump,
        too late to worry about the bump.
                Once out loud words said,
                    Too late caution tread.
                        Once, from high dive bound,
                            better hope water found.
But, when at a fork in the road
        and neither I wish to take;
                Unless backward go,
                    a path I must undertake.

For even if a decision undecided,
        it is still decided.
                Even if a choice not chosen
                        it is still chosen.

For that not settled
        will become settled.
                Its own solution will find.
                        Its own course will wind.

Be it my will or not,
        a decision will be begot.
                Be it me or another doing,
                        it will not be left brewing.

And longer left unattended,
        less easily amended.
                Longer neglected,
                        harder redirected.

For when in a scrape,
        and no way to escape;
                A pout won't get you out.

For the only way
        out of a jam,
                is to "un-jam".
                        The only way
                                out of a fix,
                                        is to fix.

When facing chaos,
        there will be chaos.
                When facing a storm,
                        there will be a storm.

You cannot

    into a problem get,
        then not expect
          a problem to be met.
            You cannot decide
              a difficult way,
                then not expect
                  a difficult day.

Jesus at fork in the road can't stay.
      One way or the other He must say.
         In the Garden, He does pray.
Too far had He gone.
    Too much had He done.
      He must finish
        what His Father had begun.
And as in the dirt He falls
     all this He recalls.
       And in the heat
         to His stumbling feet;
           once more on path He goes
              to the end that He knows.
Through the chaos
    and through the storm
      our lives to transform.
        He is not lukewarm.

So too in my journey,
           come I to roundabouts
                     with varied outs
                          and nagging doubts.
I too must resolve
           to proceed
                or to recede;
                     to go forward
                          or go rearward.
I too must pray.
           to be shown the way.
                For God has called me
                     on this trek to be.
                          This trip the Father
                               has set before me.

Stumble by stumble,
           tumble by tumble.
                Mistake by mistake
                     And if a mistake I make,
                          better then no decision take.

Station X
Jesus is Stripped of His Clothing

"Letting Go"

How does one let go
      of loved places,
           loved things,
              loved people?
How does one say good-bye,
        So long.
           Cheerio,
              All things to an end,
                    Sayonara.
How does one prepare to release
        all that is dear,
        all that has meaning,
           in this world significant,
              in this world important,
                and the people too?

Hard to do even for awhile;
        more difficult still when for good;
                when permanent.
        More intense still when no choice given;
                no option available.
        More emotional still when a person is dying;
                when ones farewells are saying;
                        final words are spoken.
For it is not only the living
        that must say good bye to the dying,
                but so too must the dying say good bye to the living.
They too must let go and prepare to leave.
        They too need to let loose everything;
                including life itself.
Setting free not only the heart and the mind,
        but the soul itself into other Hands.
                To give up the known
                        for the unknown.
                To let loose what one has
                        for what one has not yet grasped.
So much like living is dying.
        How similar the two,
                For in life a constant
                        letting go of the held.
                        A constant snatching
                                for that not yet

                        in the hand;
                for that not yet
                        in ones sure grasp.

Horizontal bars for reaching,
        one bar to the other.
            Taking hold one,
              letting go of the last.
                 Extending for the next and repeating.
Sometimes one can seize the next bar
        without letting go of the last.
            Sometimes if agile,
              one can skip a bar
                for the one beyond.
Sometimes, though, one has to swing,
        stretching for the next,
            and in mid-flight let go of the last.
              Between the bars free.
And it is here in this span of time,
        this distance of openness,
            this momentary void,
              this temporary interval,
                one has to trust;
                  one has to continue.
For once let go, no reaching back.
        Once midway, only ahead.
            The same in life.
            The same in death.
In life too, we go
     from one step to the next;
        from one phrase to another.
           Sometime knowing whats ahead
              and sometimes no notion.
And for each of us,
    varied are the gaps between;
        the distance not always certain.
          For each of us, diverse the risk taken;
            diverse the daring shouldered.

Because of the uncertainty,
　　　　　Some of us do not let go
　　　　　　　　　until firm the grip
　　　　　　　　　　　　on what is coming.
　　　　　　　　　　　　　　　Even then hesitant the letting go.
Others too freely the leap;
　　　　　not yet measured the distance;
　　　　　　　　　not yet judged the time required,
　　　　　　　　　　　　but with careless abandon the bound make.
Some of us tight our hold,

　　　　　strong our clutch;
　　　　　　　　　too concerned the slipping,
　　　　　　　　　　　　too worried the tumbling.
Only with force, pried our fingers open.
　　　　　　　Only when hard pressed
　　　　　　　　　　"un-clenched" our hands.
　　　　　　　　　　　　　For no matter how short the distance,
　　　　　　　　　　　　　　　　　too far the jump.
　　　　　　　　　　　No matter how little the risk,
　　　　　　　　　　　　　　　too great the odds.
However, some things in life
　　　　　no choice given, no options available.
　　　　　　　　　　Such it is for death.
　　　　　　　　　　　　No special exemptions provided;
　　　　　　　　　A part of our having been given breath.
　　　　　　　　　　　　A natural conclusion our coming from the womb.

And many times in our lives,
the good byes to others;
many the farewells
to those who die before us.
Many also, the good byes they to us.
Many the last words they shared.
Maybe not always noteworthy.
Maybe not even memorable,
but they shared.

Jesus, of His clothing stripped,
but also, His letting go
of family and friends.
His final words spoken;
all is now settled the best He can.
He bows His head and lets Himself die,
as He reaches for the next "bar".
We too, "bow our heads" and let ourselves die.
Letting go of one bar and reaching for the next;
and in that suspension God waits.

Jesus is Crucified

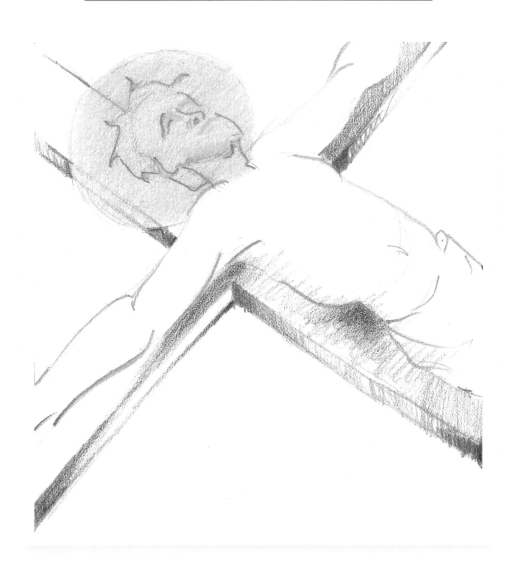

"Summation"

How does one sum up
    one's days of living?
        In a few words,
            a synopsis giving.
How does one,
    at life's earthly consummation,
        a resume provide
            in brief rumination?
Do you add and subtract
    goods and bad's?
        Do you multiply and divide
            joys and "sads"?
A formula use
    to estimate quality attribute?
        An equation of symbols
            to evaluate final repute?
How does one qualify
    one's moments and actions?
        In little time and space,
            characterize one's transactions.

How do I decide
        if my life worth
                a reference note?
                        How do I equate
                                if my breathing
                                        any difference wrote?
For some, the decisions
        seem easy to make.
                For others,
                        not so clear;
                                time it does take.
For the vast majority though,
        in between they lie.
                Not well known by many;
                        in daily living they get by.
For neither great good
        nor great evil.
                Neither great love

                nor great upheaval.
                        They are loved
                                by a few;
                                        their worth known.
                        Yet, they are,
                                by the world whole,
                                        not of renown.
So then also
        those who live alone;
                no friends or family
                        to share a home.
                                In near obscurity,
                                        they dwell.
                                In private days,
                                        their stories never tell.

Then what about those
                who have mistakes made.
                                Those in prison cells
                                and souls dismayed?
                                        Those, who from life departing,
                                                by their own choosing
                                                        the parting?

Yet, we all hope within
                not to be left "un-recalled".
                In some special way,
                                kept in mind.
                                        For some a great deed;
                                                For others a great misdeed.
                                                        For most just a need.

So how does one sum up
                one's days of living"
                                In a few words,
                                        a synopsis giving?

Perhaps, in an obituary,
                the person's attributes share.
                                Or in a eulogy,
                                        one's assets
                                                can declare.

Or at the funeral,
                the number attending
                                may indicate
                                the person's status commending.

For many,
　　just a few words engraved;
　　　　an epitaph description.
　　　　　　Or just their names chiseled;
　　　　　　　　only personal inscription.
In the end,
　　perhaps all
　　　　we can safely say
　　　　　　about another is
　　　　　　　　that he or she lived
　　　　　　　　　　and he or she died.
And perhaps that is
　　　　all we can say
　　　　　　about ourselves, too.
　　　　　　　　We lived
　　　　　　　　　　and we died.
Anything "good"
　　　　to be said
　　　　　a bonus.
　　　　　　Anything "bad"
　　　　　　　　to be said
　　　　　　　　　　unnecessary.
And along the way,
　　　　we loved some.
　　　　　　Along the way,
　　　　　　　　we couldn't.
　　　　　　　　Along the way,
　　　　　　　　　　we let God lead.
　　　　　　　　　　Along the way,
　　　　　　　　　　　　we wouldn't.

But is this
    the final rendering
        of a soul's life;
           in this world
               no longer spending?
    Is there a greater Appraiser still;
           Whose approach
             of another ilk and will?
               Whose words and sight
                  give a clearer light?
Not just of our living
        does He ascertain,
           but of our loving
             does His focus pertain.

For not the mind
      but the "heart."
         Not the body
          but the soul.
           These two remain
             when the other two go.
These two are,
      of our being, the essence.
         These two,
        of our nub,
          true existence.
So though, maybe no statue
      your likeness bearing;
         in the square
         your deeds declaring.
           With birds decorating
             and people congregating.

Nor any building tall
     your name labeled.
         Or any room small
             your memory fabled.
Not even a rare find
     to you attributed.
         Or a great discovery
             by you contributed.
No writing great
     by your hand composed.
         Nor musical score
             by you proposed.
Even if no highway
     your living recall.
         Nor by-way
             or any way at all.
But only an obituary
     your passing accounting.
         Only a brief bio
             your life recounting.
Even if only a short scribble
     on death certificate transcribed.
         Or perhaps no place
             your name inscribed.
This is not
     your life's final summation.
         Not your existence's

         bottom explanation.

That you live
    and I live;
        That for awhile we have breath;
            then comes our death.
                For awhile this world we exist;
                    then we desist.

Once, we had no life;
    then we were given life.
        Once we had no breath;
            then we were given breath.
                Born into this world a little while;
                    a chance along the way to smile.

What after that comes or not comes
    we have lived and beat our drums;
        for a moment in this universe
            we did transverse and converse.

But even more so
    in God's Hands
        our souls.
            His loving care
                our spirits consoles.
                    That is enough.
                    That will have to do
                        for me and for you.

I can ask for nothing less
    and nothing more;
        God's love for evermore.

Jesus on the cross hung;
    still in age young.
        His life as an itinerant;
            He had become an irritant.
                So here a man on a cross;
                    Another life to toss?

Station XII
Jesus Dies on the Cross

"Death"

(I not saying I am indecisive,
    far be it, for me to be so derisive;
        but, because of my kind,
            God made death a permanent bind,)

Death:
    the state of not being;
        the condition of life fleeing;
            the grim reaper,
                the permanent sleeper;
                    physical being demised;
                        our visible body down sized.

Death:
    the ultimate faith test
        or from fears and sorrows blessed.
            A foe dreaded and feared
                that our days can darken;
                    or a welcomed friend
                        in our sufferings we hearken.
Death:
    can be challenged and dared;
        an edge to life giving.
           It can be sacrificed
              and shared
                for another life living.

Romanticized and mythologized;
           death can be glamorized and glorified;
                  or vilified and horrified.
It can be lingering or unexpected.
      It can be foreseen or undetected.
           It can be sudden or self caused.
              It can at times be paused.

Some would like
    in their sleep to die;
        unnoticed with a quiet sigh.

        Others a deathbed scene;
           Loved one around,
             comforting and seen.
 Others want not alone to die;
    not by themselves to grow cold.
        But someone else make note;
           a hand to hold.

Some their death are reaping;
        their lives carelessly keeping.
                Others try their lives extending;
                        health and mind attending.
Some for death little respect
        since life a passing aspect.
                Others for dying a regard,
                        since life do not discard.

We earnestly pray
      for loved ones dying
           death not denying;
                their suffering decreased;
                    their pain totally ceased.
We may intently
      beseech God, with death
           our enemies to devour.
                For us, His aid,
                    our foes to cower.
So different "reflectives".
        So varied perspectives.
           Yet, we each, death will meet.
                All, its touch, will greet.

There are, however, many times
                in our daily living
                  "death" can also be unforgiving.
                        Many ways the spirit cries
                            before body dies.
A loved one "passes away";
        a dream decay;
          self-esteem erodes.
         a relationship corrodes,
              Hope loses hope.
                Life loses life.

Whatever it be,
 a part of us lifeless;
  a bit of us sightless.
   A void of tightness.
A taste of death
 while still inhaling.
  Taste of death
   while, yet, exhaling.
    For many, to self destruction.
     For a few, their life's final abduction.
Yes, in some way,
 "dying" affects us all.
  In some way,
   we feel its call.
    In life's little "deaths";
     reminders our last breath.

And final death, can be
 a double edge fright;
  A two fold plight.
   One is the dying itself.
    Two, what lies beyond "self"?
How will we die;
 peaceful and quickly;
  or dragged out and prickly?
   And when the body stops,
    where do we eventually drop?
Is there new life or nothingness?
  If there is nothingness
   how will we tell?
    If there be life,
     where will we dwell?
      Is there a heaven and a hell?

This is where our faith applied;
belief at this moment tried.
This, the moment of proof;
This, the ultimate time of truth.
Death is unavoidable.
It is unyielding.
It is uncompromising.
It is guaranteed.

Each our own to face.
Each our own to embrace.

For Christ,
death but an appearance of permanency.
A temporary illusion of "endency".
What seemed like death,
was but life percolating.
What seemed lifeless
was but life germinating.
For within a winter tree,
bare of greenery to see,
sap still flows quietly.
Within a bright day sky,
sunlight filled to the eye,
unseen stars the heavens beautify.

Station XIII

Jesus' Body is Taken from the Cross

"Original"

God is not
  a stand in buddy.
        He is not
           a substitute friend.
He is not a synthetic sweetener;
          not an artificial flavoring.
              He is not a surrogate beloved;
                   not an alternative "sweetheart"
                 as needed.
God is the original;
      not an imitation;
         not a carbon copy.
           He is the genuine;
              not a counterfeit.
God is a buddy.
    He is a friend.
    He is a beloved.
      He is a "sweetheart".

However, God still wants us,
        other friends to have;
                other buddies for ourselves.
He desires us
    to find other "sweethearts"
        and to have a beloved.
He does not fill in
    for what we do not have.
        He does not take the place
            of what we lack in our lives.
God is not fill dirt
    to replenish holes
        in our lives.
        He is not stuffing
            for the empty places
                in our hearts.
God does not will us
    to be alone.
        He does not wish
            for us to be
                by ourselves.

He loves so we can love.
    He cares so we will care.
        For if we shrink back
            from human love,
                our hearts will shrink.
        If we withdraw
            from life with others
                our souls will withdraw.

For there is a part of us
        that God created
            that only another human being
                can help satisfy.
      A place within us
        that only another person
            can help comfort.
      Maybe not completely,
           but still enough.
              Maybe not entirely
                but still nearly.

So don't behind God
      in terror hide.
        from love and being loved.
           Don't between His legs
              cower in fear
                your life to live,
                  Life to have.

It is the Love
    God has for us.
      It is the Life God has given us.
        Jesus did not teach God's love
           for us to tremble.
           He did not give His life
              for us to cower.

For it was friends
    who claimed Jesus' dead body.
      It was friends who took it down
        from the cross.
      It was friends who prepared
        and laid His body
          in the tomb.
        It was a friend
          who provided the tomb.

When no one else there,
His friends were.

When no one else seemed to care
Jesus' friends did.
Even in their fear
and grief,
they were there.
They stayed near.
even in confusion

So tremble if you must,
but you must risk loving
and being loved.
Cower if you need to,
but you need to wager living
to have Life.

Thus are we created
and thus are we formed.
Regardless of the pain,
love greater.
Regardless of the sorrow,
Life stronger.

Jesus' words were,
love one another
as well loving God.
Love others as ourselves
and love God

It is a package covenant;
a group pact;
a community deal.

JESUS' BODY LAID IN THE TOMB

"Darkness"

There are those times
>> when darkness overcomes us;
>>> when gloom overtakes us.
>>>> When in a cave we feel.
>>>>> When in a pit we sink.

Utter despair overwhelms our spirit;
>> total dread permeates our being.

As when the lights go out
>> and blackness left;
>>> from a nightmare awaken,
>>>> in the dark lost.

In light of day,
>> the feeling may come.
>>> In the midst of friends,
>>>> the experience may occur.

Unexpected,
> unsuspected,
>> undetected.

Your worse anxiety apparently true.
        Your secret apprehension presumably real.
                Your spirit clearly shaken.

This then is the sepulcher.
        This then the grave.
                This then the crypt.
As if buried alive,
        as if entombed breathing.
                As if light not see again.
The casket shut,
        the coffin latched.
                A hysteria in the heart,
                    A frenzy in the mind.
No seen escape,
        no way out,
            no means to flee.
From certainty of self separated.
        From God's love disconnected.
                From sense of worth isolated.
Yet, all around us, the world goes on.
        All about us, people the same,
                except for us in this time warp of our mind.

Old habits thought dead,
        back to reclaim us.
                Old addictions once more
                    to retake us.
                      Old "guilts" and doubts to "re-assault" us.

All we have gained, seems lost.
    All we have achieved, seems gone.
        All we have toiled, seems vanished,
            The ground no longer firm.
                Our footing no longer sure.

And once again, hysteria sets in;
    over again, alarm settles.
        There may be a known cause;
            Or just a subtle tweak of the soul.

The sudden realization of death;
    the abrupt end of a marriage;
        a terminal illness discovered;
            the lose of a friend or loved one.

Whatever it may be;
    whatever the catalyst;
        the stone rolled in front of the tomb.
            The grave sealed and us within.

Was our journey in vain?
    Were our efforts for naught?
        Was all our striving futile;
            a waste of a life?

An emptiness,
    a vacuum.
        Where do we turn?
          Who to help us?
Faith alone our only hold;
    trust our only salvation.
        So we cling to it.
          We grasp it tight
            until the fear passes;
              until the dread clears.

Jesus in the tomb laid.

    Christ in the grave placed.

        Though His body dead,

            He believed in the resurrection to come.

        Though His form lifeless,

           He had faith new life near.

For that we must await.

    In that we need to cling.

        In that we must grasp.

           No matter the darkness,

              God's love still there.

           Regardless the emptiness,

              we are not abandoned.

The stone will be rolled away.

    The grave will be opened.

        So hang onto hope

          no matter how frail.

           Hang onto love

             no matter how dim.

Station XV
Jesus Resurrects

"Heaven"

A great deal is said
   about heaven when
      we are dead.
         Our home to come,
            when from this world
               we succumb.

A paradise
   where believers go.
      A haven for a weary soul.
         Joyful and nice;
            already paid is the price.

No more pain or tears.
   No more illness or fears.
      Happy days unending.
         No more trials pending.
            No more sorrowful load.
               Eternity our abode.

The Beatific Vision.
    No worry or division.
        With crystals and jewels garnished.
                Streets of gold
                  and precious stones embellished.
      A home there secure.
        A dwelling place sure,
           that Jesus Himself prepared.
              No cost having been spared.
Angels with wings,
    harps and voices that sing,
        peace and what that brings,
        and all sort of that wonderful thing.
              Everlasting to God,
                our praising.
              Everlasting to Him,
                our gratitude raising.

Such a grand picture,
        this conjuring.
          An image
           so enduring.
Yet, I wonder,
    though strictly "hypothetic",
        is this description
          of heavenly life
            fully authentic?
              Or is there more
                to reveal?
              Much more
                to unseal?

Is there more
        to the heavenly Kingdom
                        than our senses,
                                its breadth,
                                        can possibly plumb?
Are these conceptions
                restraining?
                        These perceptions
                                constraining?
                                        Making God's love
                                                for us "limitive";
                                                        His Kingdom
                                                                too
diminutive.
For Paul said, what ear
                has not received;
                        what eye has not perceived;
                                such has God conceived
                                        for those who have
                                                reached life's eve.

For far greater
                God's design,
                        then we
                                can possibly define.

                        Just as the universe,
                                so immense,
                                        we cannot condense.
                        No boundaries confining.
                                No borders defining.

Is heaven more than angelic hosts
                    and decorative street?
                              More than outward appearance?
                                        More than even *bon appetit?*
Yet, I cannot lie,
          what does wait,
                    after I die,
                              is for me
                                        truly mystifying.
                                        And at times
                                                  even terrifying.
          And I probably should not
                    my time consume,
                              in trying to guess,
                                        how my next life
                                                  will resume.

And I hope God,
          I am not denying
                    with such thoughts
                              my fears prying.
                                        But still on nights alone,
                                                  when in the dark,
                                                  I ponder the thought
                                                            when from this world I
embark.
                              What lies ahead
                                        when from this world
                                                  I have tread?
And when I think
          of death being unavoidable,
                    I am forced to confess
                              a secret "foil-able".

Perhaps oblivion beyond.
                    Perhaps nothing
                              with which to bond.
Nothing spiritual;
      beyond this world physical.
                    From this world
                              no next to go;
                                        just she'ol "below".
This thought not becalming;
                    actually alarming.
                    Yet, there is
                              also the nervousness
                                        to the next world going
                                                  without a real knowing
                                        of what to expect;
                                                  upon what to reflect.
In fact,
      I am not sure,
            which is harder to accept
                    with final exhale,
                              life ended
                                        or another world
                                                  our lives extended?
And what if this world
            my soul delay?
                    Longer it wants to stay?
                              Not willing, or able, the next;
                                        for some strange reason hexed.
                    That would definitely stink;
                              trapped water in a sink.

I would find it daunting;
        very haunting;
                a spirit on the prowl;
                        would make me scowl.
Or what if reincarnated?
        Would I be frustrated?
          How many tries must I do
                 before I make it through?

And woe unto me
      if in Gehenna I end.
            What a sad place
                 eternity to spend.
                     And though, I have at times
                              God's Will tested.
                  Even at times,
                      His presence rejected.
                From God, a recluse
                      I would never choose.
                From God kept, depressing.
                    From Joy and Love, repressing.
Now I do ramble
      and my mind
        in a scramble.
            All this is but naught;
                not what I have been taught.
                      My mind fraught
                        by these thoughts.
But in the end,
      though at times fearful;
        and maybe tearful;
           however, it turns out,
              I do not want to pout.

Therefore, I must set aside
                my scattered doubt,
                        and let not my frights
                                cause such a rout.
Nor, let panic expectation
                take from me
                        hopeful anticipation.
For whether heaven is
                rhinestones and rubies
                        in silver and gold,
                                or if totally different
                                        and not as we first told,
        After all is said,

                we still do not have
                        slightest clue
                        of what lies ahead.
                                Of what will ensue.
        So vague our understanding.
                        So minute our comprehending.
To a baby in the womb,
                who is going to warn
                        what it means to be born?
                                Into a new world "thrust-ed",
                                        left behind the world once "trusted".
                                        From scratch, learning begins;
                                                new world, new things.
Yet, a child's mind
                it requires indeed;
                        where imagination totally freed;
                                and where acceptance
                                        is needed.
                                And where love
                                        goes not unheeded.

Such a heart and soul,
      with age can get lazy;
           with time can become hazy.
No longer that innocent minded;
         the power of vision
            can become blinded.
                 Limited Light.
                  Limited sight.

Yet, there are those
      in later years,
        still the eyes of a child
          the world appears.
            And what may
              have gotten jaded.
                 Once more "un-faded".

And truly blessed,
      those whose hearts
         never congealed,

           but as a youngster still,
             the mysteries of life and God
                 still revealed.

As for my own
      train of thought,
        some effort
         I require,
          once more beyond
            my small world
              to aspire.

When as a child naive
  in God I did believe.
    No hesitation.
      No reservation.
Well, in God's ways,
  I am still very naive.
    And I struggle now
      at times to believe.
Yet, as Peter did say,
  speaking for the Twelve that day,
    where else can I turn?
      Where else can I learn?
I call myself a Christian.
  And that is my position.
    Greater my belief, than my doubt.
      And that is what it is all about.

Printed in the United States
By Bookmasters